The New Novello Choral Edition

JOSEF HAYDN

The Creation
Die Schöpfung

an oratorio for soprano, tenor and bass soli, SATB and orchestra

Edited by
MICHAEL PILKINGTON

Vocal Score
(English/German)
(Mit deutschen Text und Vorwort)

Order No: NOV 072485

NOVELLO PUBLISHING LIMITED

It is requested that on all concert notices and programmes acknowledgement is made to 'The New Novello Choral Edition'.
Es wird gebeten, auf sämtlichen Konzertankündigungen und Programmen 'The New Novello Choral Edition' als Quelle zu erwähnen.

Orchestral material is available on hire from the Publisher.
Orchestermaterial ist beim Verlag erhältlich.

Permission to reproduce from the Preface of this Edition must be obtained from the Publisher.
Die Erlaubnis, das Vorwort dieser Ausgabe oder Teile desselben zu reproduzieren, muß beim Verlag eingeholt werden.

Cover illustration: the opening of "The Representation of Chaos" from the first edition of *The Creation*(1800).

Einband-Illustration: Die Eingangstakte zu "Die Vorstellung des Chaos" aus der Erstausgabe Die Schöpfung *(1800)*.

CONTENTS

PART ONE - *ERSTER TEIL*

PART TWO - ZWEITER TEIL

PART THREE - *DRITTER TEIL*

APPENDIX ONE

APPENDIX TWO
Demonstration models of secco recitatives

The soloists sing in the following movements:
Soprano: (GABRIEL) 4, 7, 8, 13, 14, 15, 18, 18a, 25a; (EVE) 27, 28, 29; 31
Alto: 31
Tenor: (URIEL) 1a, 2, 9, 11, 12, 13, 18, 18a, 22, 23, 25a, 26, 30; 31
Bass: (RAPHAEL): 1a, 3, 5, 6, 13, 16, 17, 18, 18a, 19, 20, 21, 24, 25a; (ADAM) 27, 28, 29; 31

NUMBERING OF MOVEMENTS

This new edition of *The Creation* follows the layout of the previous edition (catalogue number NOV070158) page for page, to allow this new edition to be used side-by-side with the edition it supersedes. However the numbering of movements has been changed as follows:

New Novello Edition (NOV072485)		Old Novello Edition (NOV070158)	Hoboken
	PART ONE		
1	Introduction	1	1a
1a	Recitative with Chorus	2	1b, c
2	Aria with Chorus	3	2
3	Recitative	4	3
4	Chorus with Soprano Solo	5	4
5	Recitative	6	5a
6	Aria	7	5b
7	Recitative	8	6a
8	Aria	9	6b
9	Recitative	10	7a
10	Chorus	11	7b, c
11	Recitative	12	8a
12	Recitative	13	8b
13	Chorus with Solos	14	8c
	PART TWO		
14	Recitative	15	9a
15	Aria	16	9b
16	Recitative	17	10
17	Recitative	18	11a
18	Trio	19	} 11b
18a	Chorus with Solos	20	
19	Recitative	21	12a
20	Recitative	22	12b
21	Aria	23	12c
22	Recitative	24	13a
23	Aria	25	13b
24	Recitative	26	14a
25	Chorus	27	14b
25a	Trio	27a	14c
25b	Chorus	27b	14b, d
	PART THREE		
26	Recitative	28	15a
27	Duet and Chorus	29	15b, c, d
28	Recitative	30	16a
29	Duet	31	16b, c
30	Recitative	32	17a
31	Final Chorus (with Solos)	33	17b

PREFACE

INTRODUCTION

This edition of *The Creation* attempts to provide solutions to two problems not previously addressed in one edition. First to present, as far as possible, the work clearly in the form which Haydn intended; and second to provide a version which can be sung in English without resulting in incomprehension or inviting derision. In the two most recent editions Peter Brown for Oxford University Press tackles the first problem, and Nicholas Temperley for Peters Edition the second.

There are several primary sources for the work extant. A hand-copied score, with the English added by Baron van Swieten (1733-1803), that served as the engraver's score for the first edition published under Haydn's supervision in 1800; and four sets of parts and scores used for contemporary performances some with Haydn as conductor. Haydn's announcement of the first edition has the following:

> The work is to appear in full score, so that on the one hand, the public may have the work in its entirety, and so that the connoisseur may see it *in toto* and thus better judge it; while on the other, it will be easier to prepare the parts, should one wish to perform it anywhere.[1]

Therefore the text presented here is that of this first edition, with all editorial changes clearly distinguished (see Editorial Procedure below), accepting Temperley's view that:

> It is clear that Haydn took great pains to ensure that the printed score accurately reflected his considered decisions on all details of his music and texts.[2]

There is therefore no need to go elsewhere except to confirm and correct the few mistakes that occur in the edition or to resolve ambiguities.

The situation in regard to the English words is complex. Detailed information as to the source of the anonymous English libretto and its subsequent translation and treatment by Swieten can be found in Temperley[3] and elsewhere. The sources available to the present day editor are: the first edition full score and the engraver's copy, with the English written in by Swieten, and the two English libretti published for the first London performances in 1800. It is now accepted that the latter must be based on the original, lost, English libretto. Swieten translated this into German for Haydn to set, making some modifications in the process, but attempting to keep the rhythm and accentuation of the English, so that it would be possible to add the original words later. This may explain why the German for the direct quotations

from Genesis is not to be found in any German Bible. It is strange therefore that these are the passages which cause the greatest problems when refitting the English words.

The score for *The Creation* was the first score of a major choral work to be published in two languages. Haydn knew that the work would certainly be sung in the language of the country in which performances of it took place. He wished to present an authoritative English version, following the original English libretto, and this is therefore provided here. However, there are places where Haydn and Swieten's English version is not practical for several reasons. Their command of English pronunciation and accentuation was less than reliable; the word order inversions sometimes totally obscure the sense; and there was no attempt to indicate the underlay for the lower parts in the choruses. These major gaps in the underlay of the choruses make it impossible to be certain what Haydn and Swieten intended, though it is surely the case that they intended the words to be understood by an English audience.

Clementi in his edition of 1801 attempted to solve the problems of underlay, but his solutions were somewhat unsatisfactory, and were not often followed by later editors. Sigismund Neukomm (1778-1858), a pupil of Haydn, produced one of the first vocal scores of *The Creation* under the composer's supervision. Some thirty years later in 1832, having spent much time in England, Neukomm published a revised vocal score, with English words only. In this vocal score many of the work's solecisms were corrected and some passages re-written. The subsequent 1847 translation by Vincent Novello - contained in the Novello edition of *The Creation* which this new edition supercedes - drew heavily on Neukomm's version.

Swieten's English version was attacked from the beginning. Before long editors, under the mistaken assumption that it was a fresh translation from the German, felt free to produce entirely new translations. The Eulenberg study score of 1907 had German words only, but later added a translation by Henry S. Drinker. Oxford University Press published a version by Arthur Fox Strangways and Stuart Wilson which attempts to come nearer to the language of John Milton (whose *Paradise Lost* formed the basis for much of the original). This is the translation used in the programme notes written by Donald Tovey. Breitkopf and Härtel produced a translation by Myfanwy Roberts, and Lawson-Gould of New York one by Robert Shaw and Alice Parker in 1957. All these are based on the German rather than the original English.

Addressing the omissions and distortions

of the English text left by Haydn and Swieten remains a problem for contemporary editors: Brown presents the work as far as possible as written by Haydn and Swieten; Temperley attempts to make the text completely intelligible. In this new edition I have tried to provide solutions to the problems of meaning and pronunciation, while still showing the Haydn and Swieten text, and to be careful to ensure that all editorial modifications - to text and music - can be easily identified.

EDITORIAL PROCEDURE

In the Preface to his 1832 vocal score, Neukomm wrote:

> I had the good fortune to be the pupil of Haydn for more than seven years. During that time he composed 'The Creation', and also 'The Seasons'; and he kindly permitted me to see every note of these immortal productions, from time to time, as the ideas originated; and, indeed, I arranged both compositions for the pianoforte, by his desire, and under his inspection. At that time, my design was to include, in my adaptation, the entire score. The experience, however, of thirty-three years has convinced me that the highest merit of an arrangement of this kind consists in rendering it as easy as possible, simplifying the features of the original, but without surrendering any of their spirit. It is with this in view, that I have entirely remodelled my early adaptation, and I trust that, in the form in which I now have the honour to present it to the public, it will be within the reach of every amateur of music.'

It is this piano accompaniment by Neukomm that is used in the new edition, with mistakes silently corrected from the authority of the first edition full score. Neukomm continues:

> Having so often heard this work performed under the direction of its author, and having also, on many occasions, conducted it myself in his presence, I am enabled, I hope, to render a real service to the musical world by fixing (by the metronome) the movement of all the pieces; several of which have hitherto been frequently performed in a time never intended by the composer.

These metronome marks are given here in square brackets, while dynamics have been adjusted to match the full score. Neukomm's revealing English speed indications have also been included.

The music text follows the original full score. Some modifications have been made although these have been kept to a minimum and all given in square brackets. 'Missing' slurs and dynamics have been added in simultaneous passages, but wind, brass and srings are treated independently. The main text also gives the English as it appears in the first edition, aside from cases of incorrect syllabification, where the original is given in a footnote. All missing underlay is given in square brackets to allow conductors to disagree with the solutions offered. Suggested alternative wording is given above the stave in places and where the London libretti differ from the first edition the words are given in footnotes.

Abbreviations for sources used in this edition are as follows:

score The first edition of *The Creation* published in 1800 under Haydn's supervision.
N Neukomm's vocal score of 1832.
A The libretto for 'The Creation as performed...under the direction of Mr Ashley, Sen'.
S The libretto for 'The Creation as performed...under the direction of Mr Salomon'.

Bowing in this edition not marked with a stroke is from the first edition. Where this seems impractical it is for the players, rather than an editor, to solve the problem.

Vocal slurs are given exactly as they appear in the original score. They sometimes appear merely to confirm underlay, but on other occasions seem more significant, implying *molto legato*, if not actual *portamento*. The standard appoggiaturas in recits and decorations for arias have not been added editorially, since these are, and always have been, matters for the individual singer.

RECITATIVES

The recitatives give particular problems of their own. There is nothing to be gained from altering the words of direct quotation from the King James Bible. As Tovey puts it in his fascinating essay:

> If you want to preserve Haydn's or Bach's exact notes in their recitatives you must sing them in German...recitative which does not fall into the speech rhythm of the language in which it is sung is neither speech nor language nor music.[4]

In many places it is quite clear that neither Haydn nor Swieten understood English speech rhythms. An alternative is therefore provided as an *ossia* above the stave to provide a more natural version while maintaining Haydn's barring.

Guidance for performance of recitative in Haydn's time can be found in the writings of two of his contemporaries. First C.P.E. Bach (1714-1788):

> Some recitatives, in which the bass and perhaps other instruments express a definite theme or a continuous motion...must be performed strictly

in time for the sake of good order. Others are declaimed now slowly, now rapidly, according to the context, regardless of the metre, even though their notation be barred…It can be seen in accompanied recitatives that tempo and metre must be frequently changed in order to rouse and still the rapidly alternating effects. Hence, the metric notation is in many such cases more a convention of notation than a binding factor in performance.[5]

Second, a singing guide by the London-based Italian Domenico Corri (1746-1825) has:

No particular degree of time is marked to Recitative, but it is left to the singer to prolong or shorten notes, which he ought to do agreeable to the passion and accent of the words.[6]

In the light of this guidance Appendix Two gives those recitatives which only have continuo accompaniment in a more realistic form. These are to be regarded as demonstration models, suggesting how much freedom is legitimate in performance. They may be copied and added to the cello part if desired. For both these alternative versions of the recitatives I should like to acknowledge the assistance and advice of Ian Kennedy.

SPECIFIC PROBLEMS

No. 1
Bars 77-80: English underlay only appears in the soprano in the **score**; the other parts are a note short for the text. Early editions have a pair of semiquavers in bar 79; Brown has four crotchets in bar 78; Temperley omits 'the face of'. 'On' and 'upon' were used interchangeably at the time (OED).

No. 2
Bars 53-94: some editions, including Neukomm and Temperley, give this section an A minor key signature, there is no key change in the **score**.
Bars 55, 115: 'fly' is offered for 'fled' for those who (unlike **A**, **S** or **N**) find the change to the past tense for one line a problem. See also No. 21. Note, the old Novello edition has $\frac{4}{4}$ for the original **C**.

No. 3
Bar 12: 'arise' for 'arose', as 'fly' for 'fled' above.

No. 4
Bar 10: Temperley changes 'resound' to 'resounds' on the grounds that 'praise' is the subject. But it is 'the hierachy of heaven' (a collective noun) which 'resound' the praise of God to the vaults. The first line, with the work beholding the hierachy, makes no sense, so an alternative is offered.
Bar 16: the **score** gives the second c', for *und*, and

the following bars as far as bar 22 are empty, without rests, a clear indication that the soloist should join the chorus sopranos.

No. 6
Bar 77: for 'gli-des' in the **score** Neukomm and Brown have 'glides', Temperley has 'gli-deth'.

No. 10
Bar 13: **score** has 'sta-te-ly' as three syllables throughout. If it is desired to follow the original, match the underlay with 'herr-li-cher' throughout.

No.13
Since 'The wonder of his works displays the firmament' is totally misleading, in that it is the firmament that displays the works (and not the other way around), an alternative version of the chorus is provided in Appendix One. Note, the old Novello edition has $\frac{4}{4}$ for the original **C**.

No. 15
Bar 38: Haydn and Swieten considered 'eagle' to be one syllable; either make an elision as shown, or make the second crotchet into two quavers. Note, the old Novello edition has $\frac{4}{4}$ for the original **C**.

No. 16
Bar 11: the first note in this bar is problematical. Haydn rescored this movement for the lower strings, and his final version has consecutive octaves over the barline, from *f* to *e* between Viola 1 and double bass. This seems improbable: some editors, including Brown and the Peters full score, alter the bass to *c*; others, including Temperley and this edition alter the viola to *g*.

No. 19
The textual alterations in the *ossia* are from Genesis.

No. 20
Bars 3-7: see note to No. 21 below.
Bars 35-39: the choice of rests in the **score**, and the German rhythm in bar 35 imply $\frac{3}{4}$ rather than $\frac{6}{8}$ for bars 35-37 and 39. However, the vocal rhythm in bar 37 requires $\frac{6}{8}$. It might be best to take bars 35-36 and 39 in $\frac{3}{4}$ but 37-38 in $\frac{6}{8}$, as indicated in brackets above the stave.

No. 21
Another example of mixed tenses. There appears to be some system about this as in Nos. 2, 3, 20 and 21 it is the first sentence that is in the past tense, the remainder being in the present. Thus, the first sentence sets the scene in the past, the remainder of the passage views it as it would then have been seen. However, in No. 21 *smiles* needs changing to *smiled*, since this is still part of the first sentence.

No. 25a

Bars 1, 5, 61: there is disagreement as to the melody note on beat 3 of these bars. In bar 1 both flute and clarinet have *g* in the **score**; Temperley agrees, but Brown gives *b* in his vocal score. In bar 5 the **score** and Temperley give Gabriel *g*, but Brown again gives *b*. In bar 61 the **score** gives *g* to the flute, but *b* to the clarinet and Gabriel; Temperley has *b* in the accompaniment but *g* for Gabriel, while Brown gives *b* for both. Neukomm happily follows the **score**, choosing to show the *b* of the clarinet at bar 61, but giving *g* in all other places. Brown also departs from the score at bar 77, where he argues that the *b* and *d* for the second and third quavers are an error for *g* and *b*, as given at bar 65.

No. 27

Bar 2: the **score** starts the oboe solo with a minim on the second half of the bar, but has no minim rest for the first half. Since semibreves in the score are always printed in the middle of the bar, it is much more likely that the minim is a misprint for a semibreve than that an initial rest has been omitted. Temperley's edition, which uses Clementi's reduction, has the minim; Brown (who uses a reduction by Müller) and Neukomm (used here) have the semibreve.

Bar 82: the ungrammatical sentence of the original for the chorus is here changed, following the example of Temperley.

Bar 128: 'Quarternion', in Neukomm's alternative wording, refers to the four elements, earth, air, fire and water. Since the German repeats the words 'stets neue Formen zeugt' the best solution might be 'Air, and ye elements, Nature's first born, that ceaseless changes make, that ceaseless changes make'.

No. 33

Save for the word 'would' in bar 6 the text of the *ossia* is taken from Salomon's libretto.

Michael Pilkington
Old Coulsdon. July 1998

1 *AMZ, Intelligenz Blatt* (June, 1799); trans. H.C. Robbins Landon in *Haydn: Chronicle and Works*, vol IV, p.471 (London, 1976-80)
2 Nicholas Temperley, *Haydn: The Creation* (Cambridge 1991)
3 Ibid.
4 Donald Francis Tovey, 'The Creation', in *Essays in Musical Analysis* , vol. V, p.121 (London, 1937)
5 C.P.E. Bach, *Essay on the True Art of Playing Keyboard Instruments* (1753), trans. W.J. Mitchell (New York, 1949)
6 Domenico Corri, *The Singer's Preceptor*, p. 70 (London, 1810)

VORWORT

ENLEITUNG

Diese Ausgabe des Werkes *Die Schöpfung* versucht, Lösungen für zwei Probleme anzubieten, die nie zuvor gemeinsam in einer Ausgabe angegangen wurden. Erstens, das Werk so weitgehend wie möglich völlig klar in der von Haydn vorgesehenen Form zu präsentieren; und zweitens eine Version anzubieten, die in englischer Sprache gesungen werden kann, ohne sich dem Vorwurf der Unverständlichkeit oder Lächerlichkeit auszusetzen. In den neuesten Versionen setzt sich Peter Brown im Auftrage der Oxford University Press mit dem ersteren Problem auseinander, während Nicholas Temperley im Auftrage der Peters Edition das letztere in Angriff nimmt.

Es gibt diverse Primärquellen für das Werk. Eine handkopierte Partitur mit englischen Texteinfügungen durch Baron van Swieten (1733-1803), welche als Gravurvorlage für die unter Haydns Aufsicht im Jahre 1800 veröffentlichte Erstausgabe diente, sowie vier Stimmensätze und Partituren, die bei zeitgenössichen Aufführungen, teilweise unter der Leitung von Haydn, zum Einsatz kamen. Haydns Ankündigung der Erstausgabe enthält die folgende Aussage:

> Das werk soll also ... erscheinen, und zwar in vollständiger Partitur, damit eines Theils meine Arbeit in ihrem ganzen Umfange dem Publikum vorgelegt, und so der Kenner sie zu übersehen und zu beurtheilen in Stand gesetzt, anderen Theils für den Fall, da man irgendwo das Werk aufführen wollte, die Ausziehung der Stimmen erleichtert werde.[1]

Es handelt sich aus diesem Grunde bei dem hier vorgestellten Text um den Text der Erstausgabe, wobei alle vorgenommenen Änderungen deutlich kenntlich gemacht werden (siehe nachstehende Anmerkungen zur 'Redaktionellen Verfahrensweise'), in Anlehnung an Temperleys Standpunkt:

> Es ist offensichtlich, dass es für Haydn von größter Bedeutung war, dass die gedruckte Partitur seine wohlüberlegten Entscheidungen hinsichtlich seiner Musik und der Texte genauestens wiederspiegelte.[2]

Es ist nicht erforderlich, andere Quellen in Anspruch zu nehmen. Es brauchten lediglich die wenigen in dieser Ausgabe enthaltenen Fehler gefunden und korrigiert zu werden oder gelegentliche Unklarheiten ausgeräumt zu werden.

Hinsichtlich des englischsprachigen Textes ergibt sich eine komplizierte Situation. Ausführliche Angaben zur Quelle des englischsprachigen Libretto und seiner späteren Übersetzung und Bearbeitung durch den Swieten finden sich bei Temperley[3] und an anderer Stelle. Dem heutigen Bearbeiter stehen folgende Quellen zur Verfügung: Die Partitur der Erstausgabe und die Gravurvorlage mit englischen Texteinfügungen durch Swieten, sowie die beiden englischen Libretti, die für die im Jahre 1800 in London stattfindenden ersten Aufführungen des Werkes geschrieben wurden. Es gilt nunmehr als erwiesen, dass diese das nicht mehr auffindbare englische Original-Libretto zur Grundlage haben. Swieten übersetzte dieses Original-Libretto zur Vertonung durch Haydn ins Deutsche. Er nahm hierbei einige Änderungen vor, bemühte sich jedoch, den Rhythmus und die Betonungen der englischen Sprache beizubehalten, um ein späteres Einfügen des Originaltextes zu ermöglichen. Hierdurch ließe sich erklären, weshalb der deutsche Text für die Zitate aus der Genesis in keiner deutschen Bibel zu finden ist. Aus diesem Grunde erscheint es seltsam, dass es sich ausgerechnet hierbei um diejenigen Passagen handelt, die beim Einfügen des englischen Textes die größten Schwierigkeiten bereiten.

Bei der Partitur für *Die Schöpfung* handelt es sich um die erste Partitur eines großen Choralwerkes, die in zwei Sprachen veröffentlicht wurde. Haydn wusste, dass das Werk mit Sicherheit jeweils in der Sprache des Landes, in dem die Aufführung stattfand, gesungen werden würde. Es war sein Wunsch, eine am englischen Libretto orientierte, maßgebliche englischsprachige Version anzubieten, und diese wird somit in dieser Ausgabe vorgelegt. Allerdings ist zu sagen, dass es Stellen gibt, an denen Haydns und Swietens englischsprachige Version aus verschiedenen Gründen nicht praxisgerecht ist. Ihre Kenntnisse der Aussprache und Betonung des Englischen waren nicht allzu zuverlässig; falsch angeordnete Wortfolgen machen die Textbedeutung häufig völlig unverständlich. Weiterhin wurde kein Versuch unternommen, in den tieferen Chorstimmen die gesungenen Silben den Noten anzupassen. Aufgrund dieser erheblichen Lücken in der Wortunterlegung der Chorparte ist es unmöglich, Haydns und Swietens Absichten mit Sicherheit nachzuvollziehen. Es ist jedoch ohne jeden Zweifel anzunehmen, dass sie beabsichtigten, einen für das englische Publikum verständlichen Text zu schaffen.

In seiner im Jahre 1801 veröffentlichten Ausgabe setzte sich Clementi mit dem Problem der Wortunterlegung auseinander. Die von ihm angebotenen Lösungen sind jedoch in vieler Hinsicht unbefriedigend und wurden in späteren Bearbeitungen häufig nicht angewendet.

Sigismund Neukomm (1778 - 1858), ein Schüler Haydns, erarbeitete unter der Aufsicht des Meisters einen der ersten Klavierauszüge für *Die Schöpfung*. Ungefähr 30 Jahre später (im Jahre 1832), nach ausgedehnten Aufenthalten in England, veröffentlichte Neukomm einen revidierten Klavierauszug ausschließlich in englischer Sprache. In dieser Partitur waren viele der in dem Werk enthaltenen sprachlichen Fehler korrigiert und einige Passagen völlig neugeschrieben worden. Die dann im Jahre 1847 von Vincent Novello ausgeführte Übersetzung lehnte sich stark an die Neukomm-Version an und ist Bestandteil der Novello-Ausgabe der *Schöpfung*, an deren Stelle die vorliegende Folgeausgabe nun tritt.

Swietens englischsprachige Version war von Anfang an starker Kritik ausgesetzt. Schon nach kurzer Zeit nahmen sich Bearbeiter in der irrtümlichen Annahme, daß es sich hierbei um eine freie Übersetzung aus dem Deutschen handelte, die Freiheit, ihre eigenen, völlig neuen Übersetzungen zu erstellen. Die im Jahre 1907 herausgegebene Eulenberg-Taschenpartitur hatte lediglich den deutschen Text, wurde später jedoch durch eine Übersetzung von Henry S. Drinker vervollständigt. Die Oxford University Press veröffentlichte eine Version von Arthur Fox Strangways und Stuart Wilson, in der versucht wird, der Sprache von John Milton (dessen Epos *Paradise Lost (Das verlorene Paradies)* die Grundlage für große Teile des Originalwerkes bildete) näherzukommen. Diese Übersetzung kam in den von Donald Tovey verfassten Programm-Anmerkungen zum Einsatz. Der Verlag Breitkopf und Härtel veröffentlichte eine Übersetzung von Myfanwy Roberts, während die im Jahre 1957 beim New Yorker Verlag Lawson-Gould erschienene Übersetzung von Robert Shaw und Alice Parker verfasst wurde. Alle genannten Übersetzungen basieren nicht auf der englischen Originalversion sondern auf der deutschen Version.

Die Behandlung der im englischen Text Haydns und Swietens enthaltenen Auslassungen und Veränderungen stellt zeitgenössische Bearbeiter vor verzwickte Probleme: Brown präsentiert das Werk so weitgehend wie möglich in der von Haydn und Swieten vorgesehenen Form; Temperley versucht, den Text völlig verständlich zu machen. In der vorliegenden Neuausgabe habe ich versucht, Lösungen für die Probleme mit der Sprachbedeutung und Aussprache zu finden und doch weiterhin den von Haydn und van Swieten erarbeiteten Text zu präsentieren. Ich habe mir große Mühe gegeben sicherzustellen, dass alle redaktionellen Änderungen - des Textes und der Musik - ohne Schwierigkeiten als solche zu erkennen sind.

REDAKTIONELLE VORGEHENSWEISE

Neukomm schrieb im Vorwort zu seinem im Jahre 1832 veröffentlichten Klavierauszug:

> Ich hatte das Glück, mehr als sieben Jahre lang Haydns Schüler zu sein. Während dieser Zeit komponierte er *'Die Schöpfung'* und *'Die Jahreszeiten'*, und er gab mir freundlicherweise während des Entstehens dieser unsterblichen Werke von Zeit zu Zeit Einblick in seine Arbeit, so dass ich mit jeder einzelnen Note vertraut war und das Entstehen neuer Ideen verfolgen konnte; ja, ich arrangierte sogar auf seinen Wunsch und unter seiner Aufsicht beide Kompositionen für das Klavier. Damals verfolgte ich die Absicht, die gesamte Partitur in meine Umarbeitung aufzunehmen. Meine nunmehr dreiunddreißigjährige Erfahrung hat mich jedoch zu der Erkenntnis gebracht, dass das höchste Verdienst eines Arrangements dieser Art darin liegt, das Werk so einfach wie möglich zu gestalten, wobei die Eigenschaften der Originalmusik zwar vereinfacht werden, jedoch nichts von ihrem Charakter verlieren dürfen. Unter diesem Gesichtspunkt habe ich meine frühere Bearbeitung vollkommen umgearbeitet, und ich bin sicher, dass sie in ihrer gegenwärtigen Form, die ich nun die Ehre habe, dem Publikum präsentieren zu dürfen, von jedem Amateurmusiker gespielt werden kann.'

Diese von Neukomm geschriebene Klavierbegleitung wird in der Neuausgabe verwendet, wobei noch in der Erstausgabe der Partitur enthaltene Fehler stillschweigend herauskorrigiert werden. Neukomm fährt fort:

> Ich habe dieses Werk so oft in Aufführungen unter der Leitung des Komponisten gehört und habe es in seiner Abwesenheit vielfach auch selbst dirigiert. Somit hoffe ich, dass ich der Musikwelt einen Dienst zu erweisen kann, indem ich das Tempo aller Stücke (gemäß Metronom) festlege. Viele dieser Stücke sind in der Vergangenheit häufig in einem vom Komponisten keinesfalls vorgesehenen Tempo zur Aufführung gekommen.

Diese Metronomzeichen werden hier in eckigen Klammern angegeben, während die Dynamik an die Partitur angepasst wurde. Neukomms aufschlussreiche englische Tempoangaben sind ebenfalls aufgeführt.

Die Notenschrift entspricht der Originalpartitur. Es wurden einige Änderungen vorgenommen, die jedoch auf ein Minimum beschränkt wurden und in eckigen Klammern erscheinen. 'Fehlende' Bindezeichen und dynamische Zeichen wurden in simultanen Passagen eingefügt, Bläser, Blechbläser und Streichinstrumente wurden jedoch unabhängig voneinander bearbeitet. Auch der englische

Haupttext erscheint in der Sprachversion der Erstausgabe, außer in Fällen fehlerhafter Silbentrennung, wo die Originalfassung als Fußnote angegeben ist. Fehlende Wortunterlegungen wurden in eckigen Klammern nachgesetzt, um Dirigenten die Möglichkeit zu geben ihre eigenen Lösungen einzusetzen. Alternative Textvorschläge stehen über den Notenlinien, und dort, wo die Londoner Libretti von der Erstausgabe abweichen, wird der entsprechende Text als Fußnote vermerkt. Die in dieser Ausgabe enthaltenen Abkürzungen haben folgende Bedeutungen:

Score Die im Jahre 1800 unter Haydns Aufsicht veröffentlichte Erstausgabe des Werkes *Die Schöpfung*.
N Neukomms Klavierauszug aus dem Jahre 1832.
A Das Libretto für 'Die Schöpfung in der Aufführung ... unter der Leitung von Mr. Ashley sen.'
S Das Libretto für 'Die Schöpfung in der Aufführung ... unter der Leitung von Mr. Salomon.'

In dieser Ausgabe nicht mit einem Strich markierte Bogenführungen wurden aus der Erstausgabe übernommen. Sollten diese nicht praxisgerecht erscheinen, so liegt die Lösung des Problems bei den Musikern, nicht beim Bearbeiter.

Die Bindezeichen für die Gesangsstimmen wurden unverändert aus der Originalpartitur übernommen. Während sie in vielen Fällen lediglich die Silbenanpassung zu bestärken scheinen, sind sie an anderer Stelle, d.h. dort wo sie *molto legato* oder sogar *portamento* vorschreiben, von größerer Bedeutung. Die Standard -Appogiaturen in Rezitativen und Arienverzierungen wurden redaktionell nicht verändert, da diese von jeher dem individuellen Sänger überlassen bleiben.

REZITATIVE
Die Rezitative werfen Probleme ganz besonderer Art auf. Es bringt keinerlei Vorteile, den Text der wörtlichen Zitate aus der King James Bibel zu verändern. Tovey drückt es in seinem faszinierenden Essay wie folgt aus:

> Wenn man sich genau an die von Haydn oder Bach für ihre Rezitative Noten halten will, dann muss man diese in deutscher Sprache singen ... Rezitativ, das nicht im Sprachrhythmus der gesungenen Sprache vorgetragen wird, ist weder gesprochenes Wort noch Sprache noch Musik.[4]

An vielen Stellen wird es ganz offensichtlich, dass weder Haydn noch Swieten mit den englischen Sprachrhythmen vertraut waren. Es wird aus diesem Grunde eine Alternative in Form einer *Ossia* über den Notenlinien angeboten, die einen natürlicheren Vortrag ermöglicht, jedoch die in der Originalpartitur von Haydn vorgesehenen Taktlinien beibehält.

Hinweise zum Vortrag von Rezitativen zur Zeit Haydns sind in den Schriften zweier Zeitgenossen des Komponisten zu finden: Zum einen C.P.E. Bach (1714 - 1788):

> Gewisse Recitative, whoen der Baß, oder die übrigen darzu gesetzten Instrumente entweder ein gewisses Subject. oder eine solche Bewegung in Noten haben, welche bestandig fortdauret...müssen wegen der guten Ordnung strenge nach der Eintheilung des Tactes ausgeführet werden. Die übrigen Recitative werden nach ihrem Inhalt bald langsam, bald hurtig, ohne Rückficht auf den Tact, abgefungen, od sie schon bey der Schreibart in den Tact eingetheilet werden.
>
> Man siehet wenigstens aus den Recitativen mit einer Begleitung, daß das Tempo und die Tact-Arten oft verändert werden müssen, um viele Affecten kurs hinter einander zu erregen and zu stillen. Der Tact ist alsdenn oft bloß der Scrieb-Art wegen vorzeichnet, ohne daß man hieran gebunden ist.

Zum anderen, besagt ein Gesangs-Lehrbuch des in London ansässigen Italieners Domenico Corri (1746 - 1825):

> Das Rezitativ wird mit keiner genauen Taktangabe versehen, sondern das Verlängern oder Verkürzen von Noten wird dem Sänger überlassen, der sie entsprechend der im Text zum Ausdruck kommenden Emotionen bzw. in einem anmessenen Tonfall deklamieren sollte.[6]

In Anbetracht dieser Anleitungen werden Rezitative, die lediglich eine Continuo-Begleitung haben im Appendix 2 in realistischerer Form dargestellt. Sie sollen nur als Anschauungsmodelle dienen, die zeigen, wieviel Freiheit beim Vortrag legitim ist. Sie können gegebenenfalls kopiert und dem Cello-Part beigefügt werden. Ich danke an dieser Stelle Ian Kennedy, der mir beim Schreiben der beiden alternativen Rezitativ-Versionen mit Rat und Hilfe zur Seite stand.

SPEZIELLE PROBLEME
Nr. 1
Takte 77 - 80: Die englische Silbenanpassung wird im **Score** ausschließlich für den Sopran angeboten; die anderen Stimmen haben eine Note zuwenig für den Text. Frühe Bearbeitungen haben im Takt 79 ein Paar Sechzehntelnoten; Brown hat vier Viertelnoten in Takt 78; Temperley lässt die Worte 'the face of' aus. 'On' und 'upon'

waren jener Zeit im Sprachgebrauch gegeneinander austauschbar (Oxford English Dictionary).

Nr. 2
Takte 53-94: Einige Ausgaben, beispielsweise Neukomm und Temperley, geben dieser Sektion eine A-moll Vorzeichnung, im **score** gibt es keine Tonartänderung.

Takte 55, 115: Anstelle von 'fled' wird Lesern, die (anders als **A, S** oder **N**) den Wechsel in die Vergangenheitsform für nur eine Zeile als problematisch empfinden 'fly' angeboten. Siehe auch Nr. 21. Man beachte, dass die alte Novello-Ausgabe anstelle des im Original angegebenen **C** $\frac{4}{4}$ angibt.

Nr. 3
Takt 12: 'Arise' anstelle von 'arose', aus dem gleichen Grunde wie 'fly' anstelle von 'fled' (siehe oben).

Nr. 4
Takt 10: Temperley ändert 'resound' in 'resounds' um, da es sich seiner Meinung nach bei 'praise' um das Subjekt handelt. Es ist jedoch 'the hierarchy of heaven' (ein Kollektivum), die das Lob Gottes in die Gewölbe schallen ('resound') lassen. Die erste Zeile, die besagt, dass das Werk die Hierarchie erblickt, ergibt keinen Sinn. Daher wird eine Alternative angeboten.

Takt 16: Der **score** gibt das zweite c' für *und* an, und die folgenden Takte bis zum Takt 22 bleiben leer und ohne Pausenangabe - ein klarer Hinweis darauf, dass der Solist mit den Sopranstimmen im Chor singen sollte.

Nr. 6
Takt 77: Anstelle des im **score** angegebenen 'gli-des' geben Neukomm und Brown 'glides' an, während Temperley 'gli-deth' vorschreibt.

Nr. 10
Takt 13 etc. Der **score** gibt durchgängig 'sta-te-ly' in drei Silben an. Wenn eine Anlehnung an das Original gewünscht wird, sollte die Wortunterlegung durchgängig 'herr-li-cher' sein.

Nr. 13
Da 'The wonder of his works displays the firmament' völlig irreführend ist, da das Firmament die Werke zur Schau stellt (und nicht umgekehrt), wird für diesen Satz im Appendix 1 eine alternative Version angeboten. Man beachte, dass die alte Novello-Ausgabe anstelle des im Original angegebenen **C** $\frac{4}{4}$ angibt.

Nr. 15
Takt 38: Haydn und van Swieten betrachteten 'eagle' als einsilbiges Wort; es kann entweder, wie angegeben, eine Elision vorgenommen werden, oder die zweite Viertelnote kann in zwei Achtelnoten umgewandelt werden. Man beachte, dass die alte Novello-Ausgabe anstelle des im Original angegebenen **C** $\frac{4}{4}$ angibt.

Nr. 16
Takt 11: Die erste Note in diesem Takt ist problematisch. Haydn hatte diesen Satz für die tieftönigen Streichinstrumente umorchestriert, und seine endgültige Fassung hat Paralleloktaven über dem Taktstrich, *f* bis *e* zwischen Bratsche 1 und Kontrabass. Dies erscheint zweifelhaft: einige Bearbeiter, beispielsweise Brown und die Peters Edition, ändern den Kontrabass auf *c* um; andere - u.a. Temperley und diese Ausgabe - ändern die Bratsche auf *g*.

Nr. 19
Die Textänderungen in der *Ossia* stammen aus dem Buch Genesis.

Nr. 20
Takte 3-7: Siehe nachstehende Anmerkung zu Nr. 21.

Takte 35-39: Die Wahl der Pausen im **score** und der deutsche Rhythmus im Takt 35 deuten darauf hin, dass für die Takte 35-37 und 39 $\frac{3}{4}$ vorgesehen ist und nicht $\frac{6}{8}$. Der Gesangrhythmus in Takt 37 erfordert jedoch $\frac{6}{8}$. Es wäre unter Umständen am besten, gemäß der eingeklammerten Angabe über den Notenlinien die Takte 35-36 und 39 in $\frac{3}{4}$, 37-38 jedoch in $\frac{6}{8}$ zu spielen.

Nr. 21
Ein weiteres Beispiel gemischter Tempus-Angaben. Eine gewisse Methodik in der Anwendung ist wahrscheinlich, denn in Nr. 2, 3, 20 und 21 steht jeweils der erste Satz in der Vergangenheit und der Rest in der Gegenwart. Der erste Satz setzt somit die Szene in die Vergangenheit, die dann in der restlichen Passage zur Gegenwart wird. in Nr. 21 muss jedoch zu 'smiled' umgeändert werden, da es zum ersten Satz gehört.

Nr. 25a
Takte 1, 5, 61: Es besteht eine Diskrepanz in der Melodienote auf dem Taktschlag 3 dieser Takte. Im Takt 1 wird für die Flöte und die Klarinette im **score** *g* angegeben; dies wird von Temperley akzeptiert, während Brown in seinem Klavierauszug *h* angibt. Im Takt 5 geben der **score** und Temperley für Gabriel *g* an, während Brown wieder *h* vorschreibt. Im Takt 61 gibt der **score** für die Flöte *g*, der Klarinette und Gabriel jedoch *h* vor; Temperley schreibt für die Begleitung *h*, für Gabriel jedoch *g* vor, während Brown für beide angibt. Glücklicherweise hält sich Neukomm an den **score**, wenn er im Takt 61 für die Klarinette

h angibt, an allen anderen Stellen jedoch *g*. Brown weicht auch im Takt 77 vom **score** ab, wo er den Standpunkt vertritt, dass das *h* und *d* für die zweite und dritte Achtelnote mit *g* und *h*, wie im Takt 65 angegeben, verwechselt worden seien.

Nr. 27

Takt 2: Im **score** beginnt das Oboen-Solo mit einer halben Note in der zweiten Hälfte des Taktes, hat jedoch keine halbe Pause in der ersten Hälfte. Da im **score** ganze Noten stets in der Mitte des Taktes stehen, ist es wesentlich wahrscheinlicher, dass die halbe Note irrtümlich anstelle einer ganzen Note eingetragen wurde als dass eine halbe Pause am Anfang des Taktes ausgelassen wurde. Temperleys Ausgabe, in der Clementis Klavierarrangement verwendet wird, schreibt die halbe Note vor; Brown (der ein Arrangement von Müller verwendet) und die (in dieser Ausgabe verwendete) Neukomm-Version geben die ganze Note an.

Takt 82: Der im Original für den Chor angegebene grammatikalisch unrichtige Satz wurde hier, dem Beispiel Temperleys folgend, geändert.

Takt 128: 'Quarternion' bezieht sich - gemäß Neukomms alternativem Text - auf die vier Elemente Erde, Luft, Feuer und Wasser. Da im Deutschen die Worte 'stets neue Formen zeugt' wiederholt werden, ist die bestmögliche Lösung wahrscheinlich 'Air, and ye elements, Nature's first born, that ceaseless changes make, that ceaseless changes make'.

Nr. 33 Mit Ausnahme des Wortes 'would' im Takt 6 wurde der Text der *Ossia* Salomon's Libretto entnommen.

Michael Pilkington
Old Coulsdon, Juli 1998

1   AMZ Intelligenz Blatt (Juni 1799)
2   Nicholas Temperley, Haydn: The Creation [Haydn: Die Schöpfung] (Cambridge 1991)
3   Ibd.
4   Donald Frances Tovey, 'The Creation' in Essays in Musical Analysis, [Essays in Musikanalyse] Band V, S. 121 (London 1937)
5   C.P.E. Bach, Essay on the True Art of Playing Keyboard Instruments [Essay zur wahren Kunst, Klaviaturinstrumente zu spielen] (1753), übersetzt von W.J. Mitchell (New York, 1949)
6   Domenico Corri, The Singer's Preceptor [Des Sängers Lehrmeister], S. 70 London 1810)

THE CREATION

PART I
ERSTER TEIL

No. 1

The Representation of Chaos:
Einleitung - Die Vorstellung des Chaos:

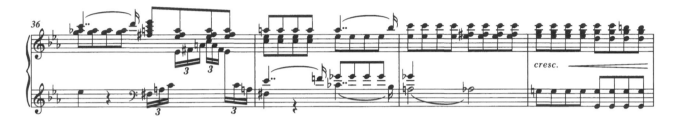

No. 1a

Recitative with Chorus
Recitativ mit Chor

*Alternatively (score) or (N)   † see Preface

No. 2

Aria with Chorus
Arie mit Chor

URIEL

Now va nish be-fore the ho - - ly beams
Nun schwan-den vor dem hei - - li-gen Strah - le

[1]

the gloom - y dis-mal shades of dark, now va - nish be-fore the
des schwar-zen Dun-kels gräu-li-che Schat-ten, nun schwan-den vor dem

ho - - ly beams the gloom - y dis-mal shades of dark;
hei - - li-gen Strah-le des schwar-zen Dun-kels gräu-li-che Schat-ten;

the first of days ap-pears, the first of days ap-pears.
der er - ste Tag ent-stand, der er - ste Tag ent-stand.

Dis - or - der yields to or - der, to
Ver-wir- rung weicht, und Ord - nung, und

or – – der fair_____ the_ place. Dis - or - der yields,
Ord - - nung keimt em - - por. Ver-wir- rung weicht,

Dis - or - der yields to or - der fair the_ place, to or - - der_
*Ver-wir- rung weicht, und Ord - nung keimt em - por, und Ord - - nung_*

fair the_ place.
keimt em - por.

No. 3

Recitative
Recitativ

Alternatively  **(N)**, see Preface

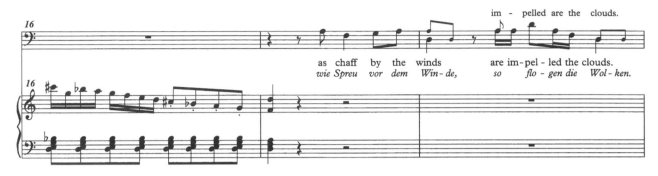

*Alternatively:

and aw-ful roll the thun-ders on

With ge - nial mois - ture now de - scend **(N)**

Now from the floods in steams a - scend re - vi - ving sho - wers of rain,
Der Flut ent - stieg auf sein Ge - heiss der all - er - quik - ken de Re - gen,

NOT slower (N)

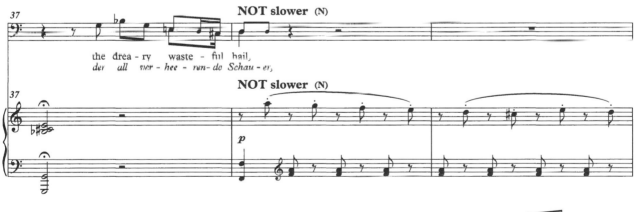

the drea - ry waste - ful hail,
der all ver - hee - ren - de Schau - er,

NOT slower (N)

the light and fla - ky snow.
der leich - te flok - ki - ge Schnee.

*streams **(A,S)**

No. 4

Chorus with Soprano Solo
Chor mit Sopran Solo

* see Preface

*'to' = 'from', bars 26 and 27 only **(score)**

20

re-sound the praise of God, and of the se-cond
er tönt des Schöp - fers Lob, das Lob des zwei - ten

vaults, and to th'e-the-real vaults re-sound the praise of God, and of the se - cond
laut er - tönt des Schöpfers Lob, das Lob des zwei - ten Tags, das Lob des zwei - ten

vaults, and to th'e - real vaults re-sound the praise of God, and of the se - - cond
laut er - tönt des Schöpfers Lob, das Lob des zwei - ten Tags, das Lob des zwei - ten

vaults, and to th'e - the - real vaults re-sound the praise of God, and of the se - - cond
laut er - tönt des Schöpfers Lob, das Lob des zwei - ten Tags, das Lob des zwei - ten

vaults, and to th'e - the - real vaults re-sound the praise of God, and of the se - - cond
laut er - tönt des Schöpfers Lob, das Lob des zwei - ten Tags, das Lob des zwei - ten

day.
Tags.

day.]
Tags.

day.]
Tags.

day.]
Tags.

day.]
Tags.

No. 5

Recitative
Recitativ

RAPHAEL

And God said: Let the wa - ters un - der the hea - ven be ga - ther - ed to - ge - ther un-
Und Gott sprach: Es samm - le sich das Was - ser un - ter dem Him - mel zu - sam - men an

- to one place, and let the dry land ap - pear; and it was so. And God call - ed the dry
ei - nem Platz, und es er - schei - ne das trock - ne Land; und es ward so. Und Gott nann - te das trock - ne

land: Earth, and the ga - ther - ing of wa - ters call - ed he Seas; and God saw that it was good.
Land: Er - de, und die Samm - lung der Was - ser nann - te er Meer; und Gott sah, dass es gut war.

No. 6

Aria
Arie

Allegro assai [♩=138]

clouds their tops as - cend.
Gip - - - fel steigt em - por.

ver - dant (N)
Thro' th'o - pen plains out - stretch - ing
Die Flä - che, weit ge - dehnt, durch-

wide in ser - pent er - ror ri - vers flow.
- läuft der brei - te Strom in man - cher Krüm - me.

Thro'
Die

ver - dant (N)
th'o - pen plains out - stretch - ing wide, out - stretch - ing wide
Flä - che, weit ge - dehnt, durch - läuft der brei - te Strom

in ser - pent er - ror, in ser - - - - - - - - - pent
in man - cher Krüm - me, durch - läuft

26

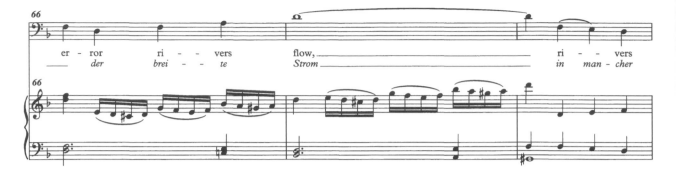

er - ror ri - - vers flow,_____ ri - - vers
_____ der brei - - te Strom_____ in man - cher

flow._____
Krüm - - - - - - - me.

N.B. Always the same movement to the End, and NOT slower (N)

† Soft - - - ly pur - - - ling__ *glides
Lei - - - se rau - - - schend_ glei - - - tet

N.B. Always the same movement to the End, and NOT slower (N)

on thro' si - - lent vales the lim - - pid
fort, im stil - - len Tal der hel - - le

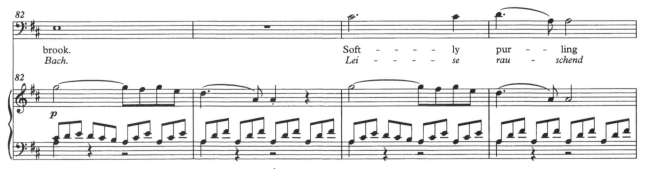

brook. Soft - - - ly pur - - ling
Bach. Lei - - - se rau - schend

* **score** makes 'gli-des' two syllables throughout, see Preface.   † In silent vales soft gliding brooks by gentle noise mark out their way. **(A,S)**

glides _____ on,   thro' si - - lent vales the
glei - - - - - - tet fort,   *im stil - - len Tal der*

4

lim - - pid brook.   Soft - - ly pur - - ling
hel - - le Bach.   *Lei - - se rau - - schend*

glides _____ on   thro' si - lent vales the
glei - - tet fort,   *im stil - - len Tal der*

lim - - pid brook.   Soft - - - ly
hel - - le Bach.   *Lei - - - se*

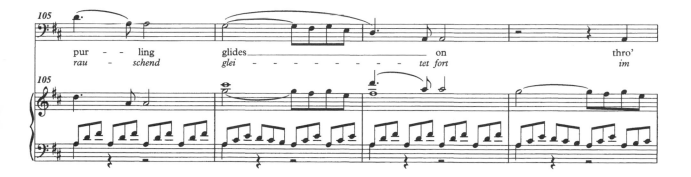

pur - ling glides _____ on   thro'
rau - schend glei - - - - - - tet fort   *im*

NOT slower (N)

si - - - lent vales___ the lim - - pid brook,
stil - - - len Tal___ der hel - - le Bach,

thro' si - - lent vales the lim - - pid brook.
im stil - - len Tal der hel - - le Bach.

No. 7

Recitative
Recitativ

bring forth grass, the herb yield - ing

GABRIEL

And God said: Let the earth bring forth grass, the herb yield - ing
Und Gott sprach: Es brin - ge die Er - de Gras her - vor, Kräu - ter, die Sa - men

yield - ing fruit af - ter his kind,

seed, and the fruit tree yield - ing fruit af - ter his kind,
ge - ben, und Obst - bäu - me, die Früch - te brin - gen ih - rer Art ge - mäss,

in it - self, u - pon the earth: and it was so.

whose seed is in it - self u - pon the earth; and it was so.
die ih - ren Sa - men in sich selbst ha - ben auf der Er - de; und es ward so.

No. 8

Aria
Arie

With ver - dure clad the
Nun beut die Flur das

fields ap - pear de - light - ful to the ra - vish'd sense; by flo - wers sweet and gay
fri - sche Grün dem Au - ge zur Er - göt - zung dar; den an - muts - vol - len Blick

en - han - ced is the char - ming sight, en - han - ced
er - höht der Blu - men sanf - ter Schmuck, er - höht der

is the char - ming sight.
Blu - men sanf - ter Schmuck.

Here vent their fumes the
Hier duf - ten Kräu - ter

fra - grant herbs, here shoots the heal - ing plant, here shoots the heal - ing plant,
Bal - sam aus; hier sprosst den Wun - den Heil, hier sprosst den Wun - den Heil,

here shoots the heal - ing plant,_____ the_ heal - ing
hier sprosst den Wun - den Heil,_____ den_ Wun - den

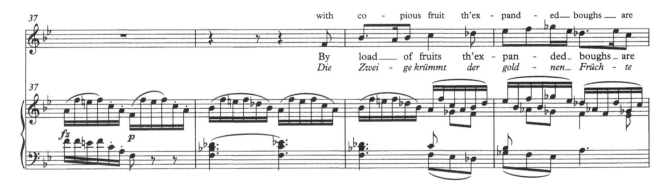

plant,_____
Heil,_____

here shoots_ the heal - - ing plant.
hier sprosst_ den Wun - - den Heil.

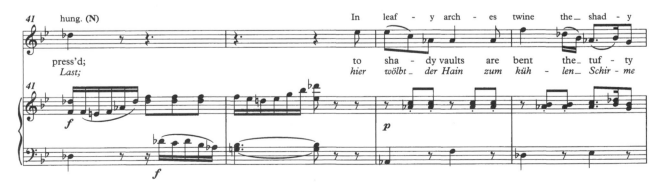

with co - pious fruit th'ex - pand - ed_ boughs_ are

By load_ of fruits th'ex - pan - ded_ boughs_ are
Die Zwei - ge krümmt der gold - nen_ Früch - te

hung. (N)

In leaf - y arch - es twine the_ shad - y

press'd;
Last;

to sha - dy vaults are bent the tuf - ty
hier wölbt_ der Hain zum küh - len Schir - me

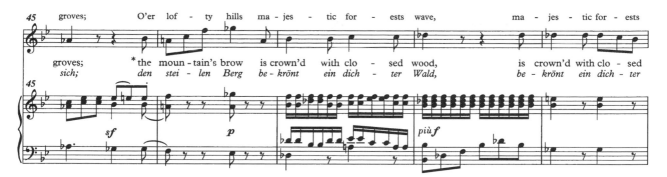

* with clos-ed wood is crowned the moun-tain's brow. **(A,S)**

fra - grant herbs, here shoots the heal - ing plant,
Bal - sam aus; hier sprosst den Wun - den Heil,

here shoots the heal - - ing plant.
hier sprosst den Wun - - den Heil.

Here vent their fumes the fra - grant herbs, here shoots the heal - ing plant,
Hier duf - ten Kräu - ter Bal - sam aus; hier sprosst den Wun - den Heil,

the heal - ing plant, the heal - ing plant, here
den Wun - den Heil, den Wun - den Heil, hier

shoots the hea - ling plant.
sprosst den Wun - den Heil.

34

*score makes 'sta-te-ly' three syllables throughout, see Preface.

38

No. 11

Recitative
Recitativ

No. 12

Recitative
Recitativ

*Alternatively:

with thou-sand, thou-sand stars   that then ap-pear'd spang-ling the vault of heaven.

No. 13

Chorus with Solos *
Chor mit Soli

*see Preface and Appendix One.

46

PART TWO
ZWEITER TEIL

No. 14

Recitative
Recitativ

Allegro
GABRIEL

And God said:
Und Gott sprach:

Let the wa- ters bring forth a-
Let the wa- ters bring forth a- bun- dant-
Es brin- ge das Was- ser in der Fül- le her-

that hath life,
-bun- dant- ly
-ly the mov- ing crea- ture that hath life, and fowl
-vor we- ben- de Ge- schöp- fe, die Le- ben ha- ben, und Vö- gel, die

of hea- ven.
that may fly a- bove the earth in the o- pen fir- ma- ment of heaven.
ü- ber der Er- de flie- gen mö- gen in dem of- fe- nen Fir- ma- men- te des Him- mels.

No. 15

Aria
Arie

Moderato [♩=126]

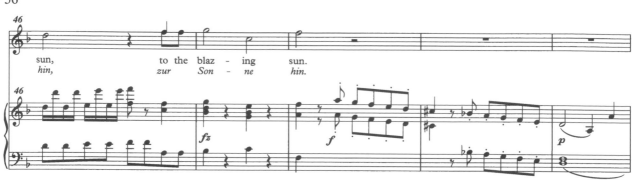

sun, to the blaz - ing sun.
hin, zur Son - ne hin.

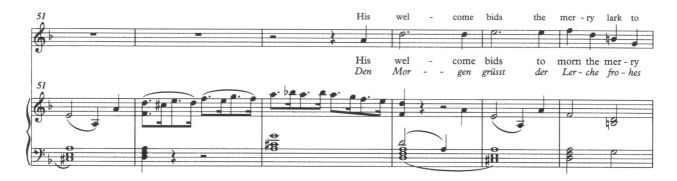

His wel - come bids the mer - ry lark to
His wel - come bids to morn the mer - ry
Den Mor - gen grüsst der Ler - che fro - hes

morn, his wel - come bids the mer - ry lark to
lark, his wel - come bids to morn the mer - ry
Lied, den Mor - gen grüsst der Ler - che fro - hes

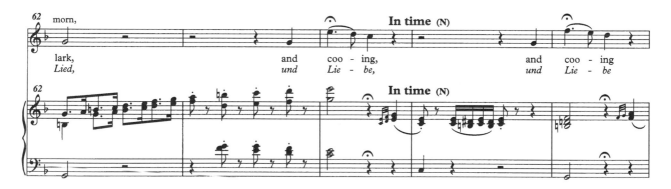

morn,
lark, and coo - ing, and coo - ing
Lied, und Lie - be, und Lie - be

In time (N)

calls_ the ten - der dove his mate, calls_ the ten - der dove his mate,
girrt_ das_ zar - te Tau - ben-paar, girrt_ das_ zar - te Tau - ben-paar,

calls_ the_ ten-der dove his mate.]
girrt_ das_ zar - te Tau - ben-paar,
[and coo - ing, and coo - ing
und Lie - be, und Lie - be

calls the ten-der dove his mate,
girrt das zar-te Tau-ben-paar,
calls the ten - - der dove_____ his
girrt das zar - - te_ Tau - - ben-

mate,] the ten - - - - - - - - - - - - - - - der_
*-paar, das zar - - - - - - - - - - - - - - te_*

dove his mate.
Tau - ben - paar.

From ev-'ry bush _____ and grove re-
_Aus je-dem Busch _____ und Hain er-_

-sound the night-in-gale's de-light-----ful notes.
-schallt der Nach-ti-gal----len sü-sse Keh----le.

No _____ grief af-
Noch drück-te

-fect-ed yet her breast, nor _____ to a mourn-ful tale were
Gram nicht ih-re Brust, noch war zur Kla-ge nicht ge-

tun'd her soft, _____ her soft en-chant-ing
-stimmt ihr rei-zen-der, ihr rei-zen-der Ge-

lays,
- sang,
her soft
ihr rei - - - - - - - - -

en - chant - ing,
- - - - - - - - zen- der,
her soft en-chant-ing lays.
ihr rei-zen-der Ge - sang.

No grief af - fect-ed yet her breast,
Noch drück-te Gram nicht ih - re Brust,
nor to a mourn-ful tale were
noch war zur Kla - ge nicht ge -

tun'd
- stimmt
her soft,
ihr rei - zen-der,
her soft en-chant-ing lays,
ihr rei - zen-der Ge - sang,

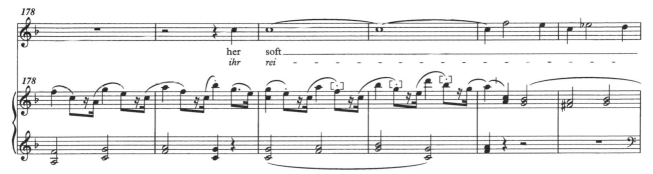

her soft _____
ihr rei _ _ _ _ _ _ _ _ _ _ _ _

____ en - chant - ing ___ lays, her soft _____
- zen-der ___ Ge - sang, ihr rei _ _ _ _

_____ en - chant ____ ing lays, her
_ _ _ _ _ _ _ _ _ _ _ _ zen - der ___ Ge - sang, ihr

soft en - chant-ing ___ lays, her ____ soft en - chant-ing ___ lays.
rei - zen-der ___ Ge - sang, ihr ____ rei - zen-der ___ Ge - sang.

No. 16

Recitative

Recitativ

* see Preface   † Be multiplied ye finny tribes (A,S)

fill each wa - t'ry deep. / *fül - let je - de Tie - fe!* Be fruit - ful, grow and mul - ti - ply! / *Seid frucht - bar, wach - set, meh - ret euch!* And / *Er-*

in your God and Lord re - joice, and in your God and Lord re - joice! / *- freu - et euch in eu - rem Gott, er - freu - et euch in eu - rem Gott!*

No. 17

Recitative
Recitativ

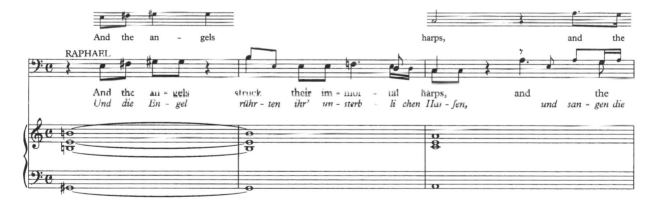

And the an - gels harps, and the

RAPHAEL

And the an - gels struck their im - mor - tal harps, and the / *Und die En - gel rühr - ten ihr' un - sterb - li chen Har - fen, und san - gen die*

won - ders,

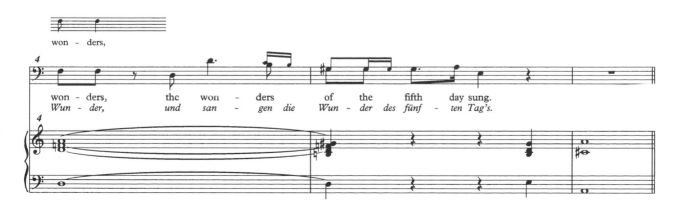

won - ders, the won - ders of the fifth day sung. / *Wun - der, und san - gen die Wun - der des fünf - ten Tag's.*

64

No. 18

Trio: Chorus with Solos
Terzett: Chor mit Soli

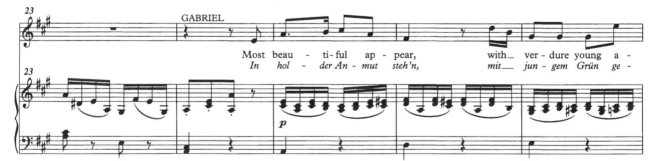

Their nar - row sin - uous veins dis - til in crys - tal drops, the
Aus ih - ren A - dern quillt, in flie - ssen - dem Kri - stall, der

foun - tain
foun - tain, the foun - tain fresh and bright. Their nar - row sin - uous
küh - len - de, der küh - len - de Bach her - vor. Aus ih - ren A - dern

veins dis - til in crys - tal drops the foun - tain fresh and bright.
quillt, in flie - ssen - dem Kri - stall, der küh - len - de Bach her - vor.

URIEL

In lof - ty cir - cles plays, and ho - vers thro' the sky, the
In fro - hen Krei - sen schwebt, sich wie - gend in der Luft, der

cheer - ful (N) cheer - ful (N) And
cheer - ful host of birds, the cheer - ful host of birds. And
mun - te - ren Vö - gel Schar, der mun - te - ren Vö - gel Schar. Den

*Both notes given in **score**

[Attacca]

No. 18a

Chorus with Solos
Chor mit Soli

*The Lord is great, His glory lasts for ever and evermore (A,S)

No. 19

Recitative
Recitativ

No. 20

Recitative
Recitativ

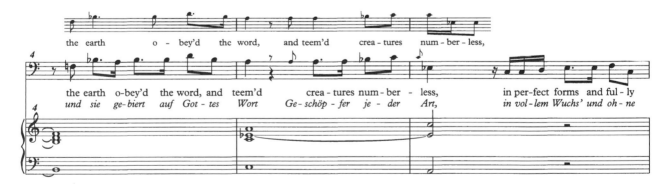

* see Preface

*see Preface

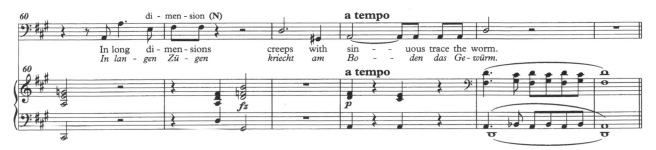

No. 21

Aria
Arie

RAPHAEL

*Now heav'n in
Nun scheint in

full - est glo - - ry shone;
vol - lem Glan - ze der Him - mel.

smiled (N)

earth † smiles in
Nun prangt in

all her rich at - tire.
ih - rem Schmuk - ke die Er - de.

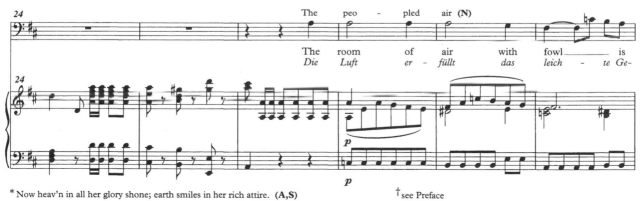

The peo - pled air (N)

The room of air with fowl is
Die Luft er - füllt das leich - te Ge-

* Now heav'n in all her glory shone; earth smiles in her rich attire. **(A,S)**   † see Preface

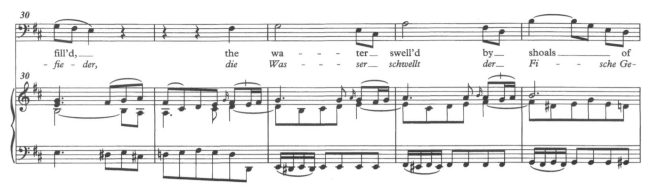

fill'd,   the wa - - - ter swell'd by shoals   of
- fie - der,   die Was - - - ser schwellt der Fi - - sche Ge-

fish;   by hea - vy beasts the ground is trod,
- wim - mel;   den Bo - - den drückt der Tie - - re Last,

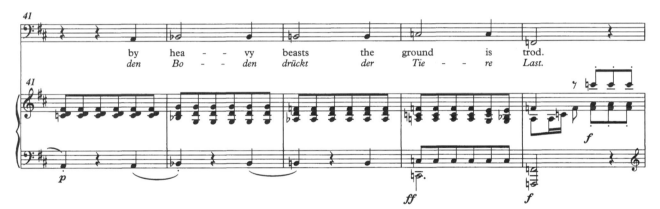

by hea - vy beasts the ground is trod.
den Bo - - den drückt der Tie - - re Last.

But all the
Doch war noch

work was not com - plete,   but all the work was not com - plete.   There want - ed
al - les nicht voll - bracht,   doch war noch al - les nicht voll - bracht.   Dem Gan - zen

yet that won-d'rous be - ing, that grate - ful should God's pow'r ad - mire,
fehl - te das Ge-schöpf, das Got - tes Wer - - ke, dank - - bar seh'n,

with heart and voice his goodness
des Her - - ren Gü - te prei - sen

praise. But all the work was not com-plete. There wan-ted
soll. Doch war noch al - les nicht voll-bracht. Dem Gan-zen

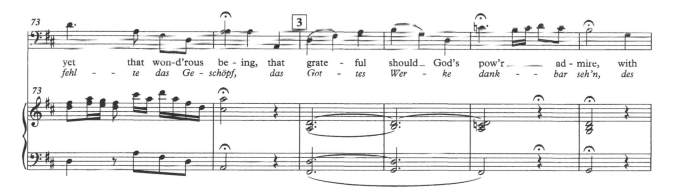

yet that won-d'rous be - ing, that grate - ful should God's pow'r ad - mire, with
fehl - te das Ge-schöpf, das Got - tes Wer - ke dank - - bar seh'n, des

heart and voice his good - ness praise, that
Her - ren Gü - te prei - sen soll, das

grate - - ful should __ God's pow'r ad - mire, with heart and voice with
Got - tes Wer - ke dank - bar seh'n des Her - ren Gü - te

heart, _____ sen __ soll, with heart and voice _____ his
prei - - - - - - - - sen __ soll, des Her - ren Gü - te prei - - -

good - - ness __ praise, with heart and voice, __ with
- - - sen __ soll, des Her - ren Gü - te, des

heart and voice his __ good - - ness praise.
Her - ren Gü - te __ prei - - sen __ soll.

No. 22

Recitative
Recitativ

URIEL

So God cre-a-ted man in his own im-age. In the im-age of

And God cre-a-ted man in his own im-age. In the im-age of
Und Gott schuf den Men-schen nach sei-nem E- ben-bil-de. Nach dem E-ben-bil-de

God cre-a-ted he him. He breathed in-to his

God cre-a-ted he him. Male and fe-male cre-a-ted he them. He breath-ed
Got-tes schuf er ihn. Mann und Weib er-schuf er sie. Den A- tem des

nos-trils the breath of life, and man

in to his nos-trils the breath of life, and man be-came a liv-ing soul.
Le- bens hauch-te er in sein An-ge-sicht, und der Mensch wur-de zur le-ben-di-gen See- le.

No. 23

Aria
Arie

Andante [♩=108]

URIEL

In na-tive worth and ho-nour clad, with beau-ty, cou-rage,_
Mit Würd' und Ho- heit an - ge-tan, mit Schön-heit, Stärk' und___

strength a-dorn'd, to heav'n e-rect and tall he stands a man, *the
Mut be-gabt, gen Him-mel auf-ge-rich- tet, steht der Mensch, ein

Lord and King of na-ture all.
Mann und Kö-nig der Na-tur.

His loft-y and ex-pand-ed brow (N)

The large and arch-ed front sub-lime
Die breit ge-wölbt' er-hab'- ne Stirn,

of wis-dom deep de-clares the seat, and
ver-künd't der Weis-heit tie- fen Sinn, und

in his eyes with bright- ness †shines the soul, the
aus dem hel-len Blik- ke strahlt der Geist, des

*The Lord of earth and Nature's king (A,S)   † shone (A,S)

breath and i - - - mage of his God.
Schöp - - - fers Hauch und E - - ben - bild.

And
Und

in his eyes with bright - - - ness shines the
aus dem hel - len Blik - - ke strahlt der

soul, the breath and i - - - mage of his
Geist, des Schöp - - - fers Hauch und E - - - ben-

God.
- bild.

No. 24

Recitative
Recitativ

And God saw ev-'ry-thing that he had made; and be-hold, it was ve-ry

RAPHAEL

And God saw ev-'ry-thing, that he had made; and be-hold, it was ve-ry
Und Gott sah je-des Ding, was er ge-macht hat-te; und es war sehr

good;

thus closed the sixth day.

good; and the hea-ven-ly choir in song di-vine thus clo-sed the sixth day.
gut; und der himm-li-sche Chor fei-er-te das En-de des sech-sten Ta-ges mit lau-tem Ge-sang.

No. 25

Chorus
Chor

Vivace [♩=104]

SOPRANO

A-chiev-ed is the glo-rious work,
Vol-len-det ist das gro-sse Werk,

ALTO

[A-chiev-ed is the glo-rious work, the
Vol-len-det ist das gro-sse Werk, der

TENOR

[A-chiev-ed is the glo-rious work,]
Vol-len-det ist das gro-sse Werk,

BASS

[A-chiev-ed is the glo-rious work, the
Vol-len-det ist das gro-sse Werk, der

be the praise of God! In lof-ty strains let us re-
Lob sei un - - ser Lied! Auch uns-re Freud' er-schal - le

be the praise of God! In lof-ty strains let us re-
Lob sei un - ser Lied! Auch uns-re Freud' er-schal - le

be the praise of God! In lof-ty strains let us re-
Lob sie un - ser Lied! Auch uns-re Freud' er-schal - le

be the praise of God! In lof-ty strains let us re-
Lob sei un - - ser Lied! Auch uns-re Freud' er-schal - le

- joice! Our song let be the praise of God, the praise of God, the praise of God!
laut! Des Her-ren Lob sei un - ser Lied, sei un - ser Lied, sei un - ser Lied!

- joice! Our song let be the praise of God, the praise of God, the praise of God!]
laut! Des Her-ren Lob sei un - ser Lied, sei un - ser Lied, sei un - ser Lied!

- joice! Our song let be the praise of God, the praise of God, the praise of God!]
laut! Des Her-ren Lob sei un - ser Lied, sei un - ser Lied, sei un - ser Lied!

- joice! Our song let be the praise of God, the praise of God, the praise of God!]
laut! Des Her-ren Lob sei un - ser Lied, sei un - ser Lied, sei un - ser Lied!

No. 25a

Trio
Terzett

*see Preface   †Gabriel has | ♩ ♩ ⅞ ♫ | (sic) in **score**   ** Uriel has | ♩ ♩ ⅞ ♩ | (sic) in **score**

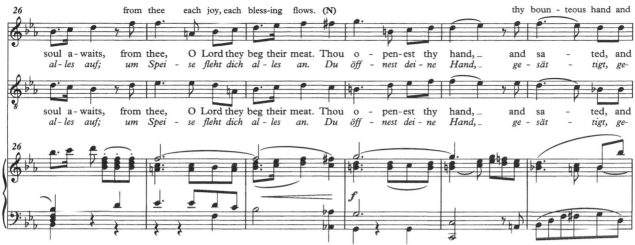

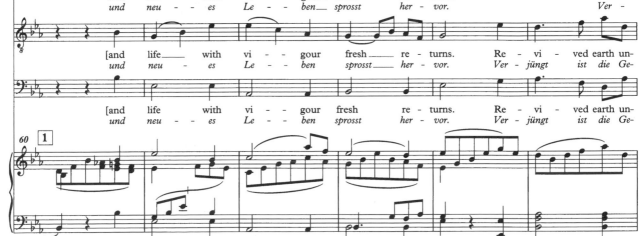

[Attacca]

No. 25b

Chorus
Chor

*On high exalted reigns the Lord. (A,S)   †'Hallelujah' for 'Alleluia' throughout (S,N)

END OF PART II

PART THREE
DRITTER TEIL

No. 26

Recitative
Recitativ

URIEL Recit.

man - tle

In ro - sy mantle ap-
Aus Ro - sen - wol - ken bricht, ge-

Duet and Chorus
Duett und Chor

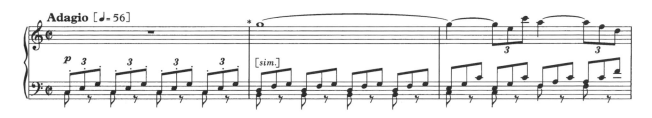

*see Preface   †The heav'n and earth are filled.   This world, so wondrous and so great, **(A,S)**

*Adam rhythm ♩. ♪♪ in **score**.

* In your extended course proclaim the glorious power of the Lord. **(A,S)**   † th'almighty pow'r and praise of God **(score)**, see Preface

*Alternatively:

Air, and ye e-le-ments, Na-ture's first born, that in qua-ter-nion run, and cease-less chan-ges make,

(N) see Preface

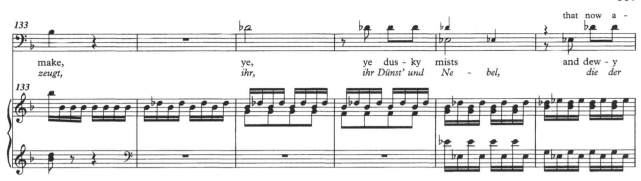

* 'raise' = 'rise' (A,S)

*His name is great, (A,S)

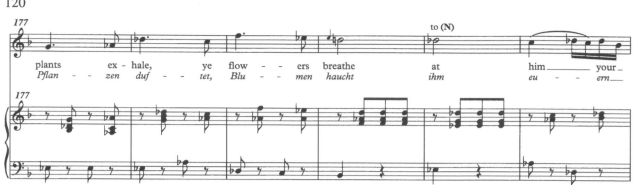

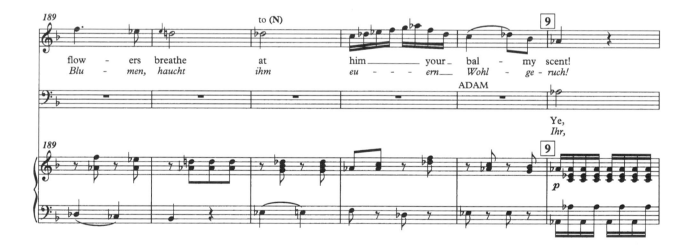

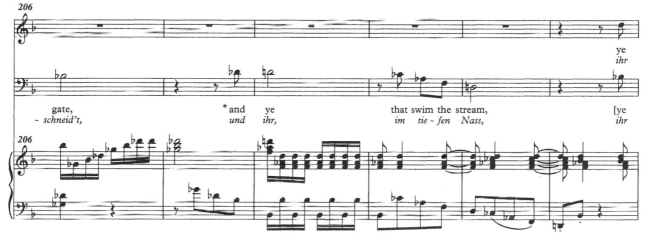

*Ye that thro' waters glide (A,S)

*ev'n (score, A,S,N)

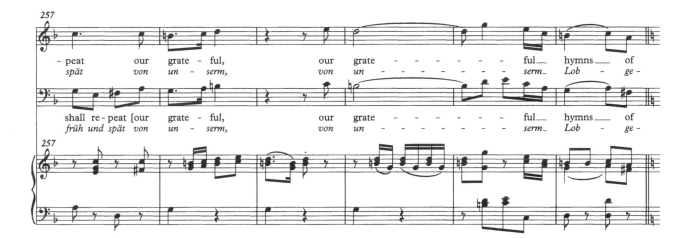

* Thy pow'r adore the earth and heaven (A,S)

130

No. 28

Recitative
Recitativ

*two syllables (score)

No. 29

Duet
Duett

* two syllables throughout **(score)**

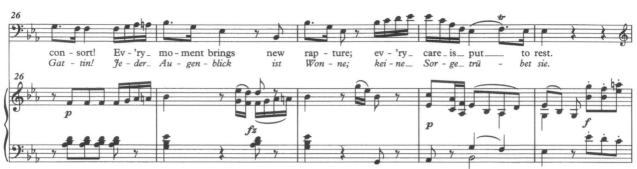

con - sort! Ev - 'ry mo - ment brings new rap - ture; ev - 'ry care is put to rest.
Gat - tin! Je - der Au - gen - blick ist Won - ne; kei - ne Sor - ge trü - bet sie.

1 EVE

Spouse a - dor - ed! At thy side pur - est
Teu - rer Gat - te! Dir zur Sei - te schwimmt in

Life and all its pow'rs, all I
joys o'er - flow the heart. Life and all I am, all I
Freu - den mir das Herz. Dir ge - wid - met ist mein

have is thine, (N)
am is thine, my re - ward, my re - ward thy love shall
Le - ben, dei - ne Lie - be, dei - ne Lie - be sei mein

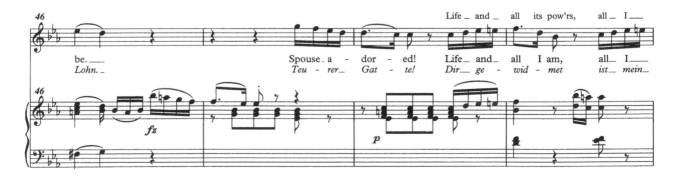

be. Spouse a - dor - ed! Life and all I am, all I
Lohn. Teu - rer Gat - te! Dir ge - wid - met ist mein

* what is it to me (A,S)

* hour (A,S)   † To thee be vow'd it whole (A,S)

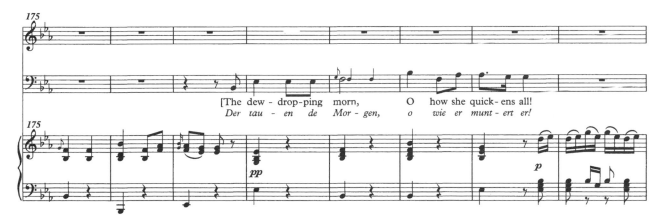

208

[what is to me]
was wä - re mir

[the breath of ev'n,]
der A - bend hauch,

thee, what is to me]
dich, was wä - re mir

[the morn-ing dew,]
der Mor - gen thau,

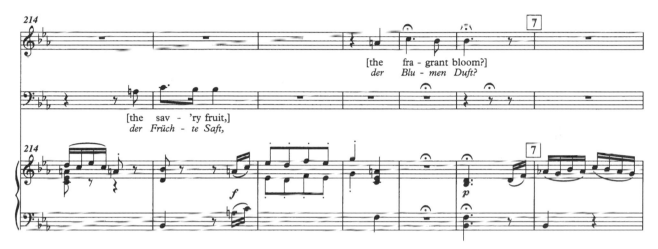

214

[the fra - grant bloom?]
der Blu - men Duft?

7

[the sav - 'ry fruit,]
der Früch - te Saft,

221

[With thee, with thee is ev-'ry joy en-han - ced;]
Mit dir, mit dir er - höht sich je - de Freu - de;

[with
mit

[With thee, with thee is ev'ry joy en-han - ced;]
Mit dir, mit dir er - höht sich je - de Freu - de;

[with
mit

228

thee, with thee de - light is e - ver new;]
dir, mit dir ge - neiss' ich dop - pelt sie;

8

[with thee, —
mit dir,—

thee, with thee de - light is e - ver new;]
dir, mit dir ge - neiss' ich dop - pelt sie;

[with thee,
mit dir,

No. 30

Recitative
Recitativ

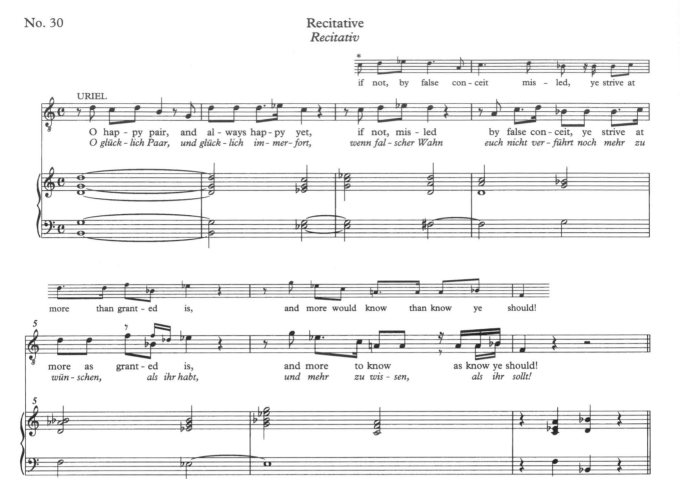

No. 31

Final Chorus (with Solos)
Schlusschor (mit Soli)

* see Preface   † ye all, (score, A),   all ye (S)

*Let on high resound his name (A)　　　　†ever (A)

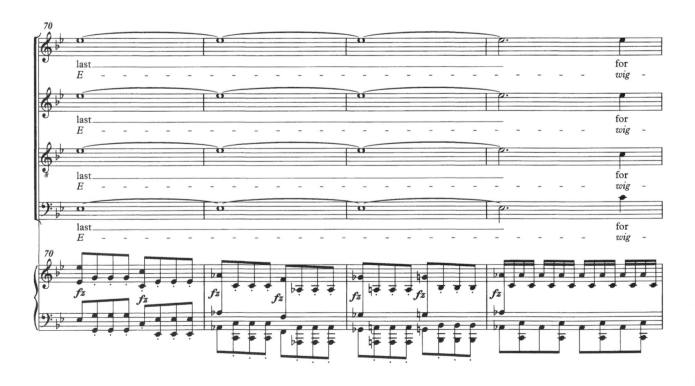

Published by Novello Publishing Limited
Music setting by Stave Origination

APPENDIX ONE

No 13 Trio and Chorus

Alternative version

e - ver, e - - ver un - der - stood, e - ver, e - ver,

e - ver, e - - ver un - der - stood, e - ver, e - ver,

e - ver, e - - ver un - - der - stood, e - ver, e - ver,

Più allegro 3

e - - - ver, _____ e - - ver un - der - stood.

e - - ver, e - - ver un - der - stood.

e - ver, e - - ver un - - der - stood.

Più allegro 3

The hea - vens are

The hea - vens are

The hea - vens are tell - ing the

The hea - vens are tell - ing the

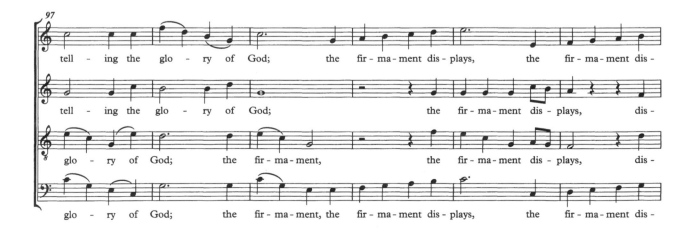

tell - ing the glo - ry of God; the fir - ma - ment dis - plays, the fir - ma - ment dis -

tell - ing the glo - ry of God; the fir - ma - ment dis - plays, dis -

glo - ry of God; the fir - ma - ment, the fir - ma - ment dis - plays, dis -

glo - ry of God; the fir - ma - ment, the fir - ma - ment dis - plays, the fir - ma - ment dis -

plays the won-der of his works.

plays the won-der of his works.

plays the won-der of his works.

plays the won-der of his works.

The fir-ma-ment dis-plays the won-der, the

The fir-ma-ment dis-plays the won-der of his works, the won-der of his

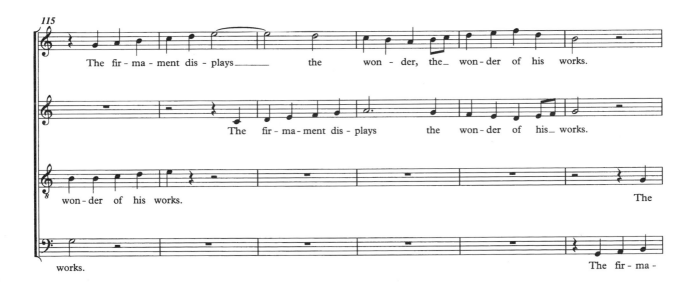

The fir-ma-ment dis-plays the won-der, the won-der of his works.

The fir-ma-ment dis-plays the won-der of his works.

won-der of his works. The

works. The fir-ma-

APPENDIX TWO

Creation - Recits.
Appendix Version

So God cre-a-ted man in his own im-age, in the im-age of God cre-a-ted he him; male and fe-male cre-a-ted he them. He breathed in-to his nos-trils the breath of life; and man be-came a liv-ing soul.

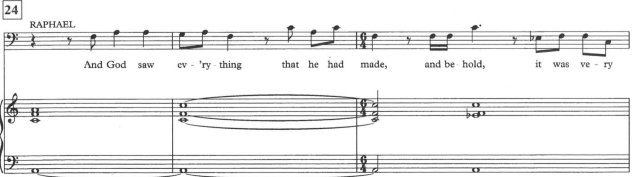

And God saw ev-'ry-thing that he had made, and be-hold, it was ve-ry

168

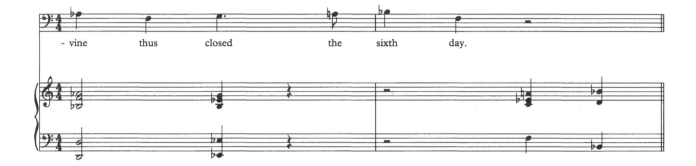

30